JOHN F. KENNEDY'S
INAUGURAL ADDRESS

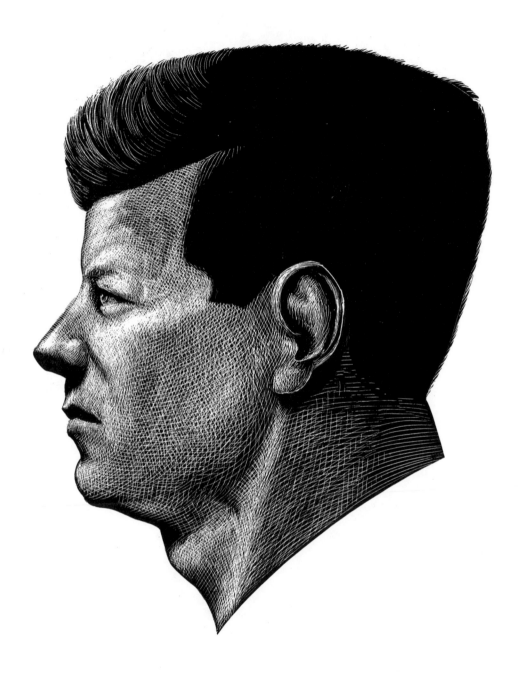

The FIRST BOOK EDITION of

JOHN F. KENNEDY'S
INAUGURAL ADDRESS

Proclamation by Lyndon B. Johnson

Illustrated by Leonard Everett Fisher

FRANKLIN WATTS, INC.
575 Lexington Avenue, New York 22

FIRST PRINTING
Library of Congress Catalog Card Number: 64-25631
Illustrations copyright © 1964
by Franklin Watts, Inc.
Printed in the United States of America
by Polygraphic Co. of America, Inc.

THE GIFT OUTRIGHT

The land was ours before we were the land's.
She was our land more than a hundred years
Before we were her people. She was ours
In Massachusetts, in Virginia,
But we were England's, still colonials,
Possessing what we still were unpossessed by,
Possessed by what we now no more possessed.
Something we were withholding made us weak
Until we found out that it was ourselves
We were withholding from our land of living,
And forthwith found salvation in surrender.
Such as we were we gave ourselves outright
(The deed of gift was many deeds of war)
To the land vaguely realizing westward,
But still unstoried, artless, unenhanced,
Such as she was, such as she would become.

Robert Frost

The White House

INAUGURAL ADDRESS
of
PRESIDENT JOHN F. KENNEDY

As Actually Delivered

We observe today . . . a celebration of freedom . . .

Vice President Johnson, Mr. Speaker, Mr. Chief Justice, President Eisenhower, Vice President Nixon, President Truman, Reverend Clergy, Fellow Citizens:

We observe today not a victory of party but a celebration of freedom—symbolizing an end as well as a beginning—signifying renewal as well as change. For I have sworn before you and Almighty God the same solemn oath our forebears prescribed nearly a century and three quarters ago.

The world is very different now. For man holds in his mortal hands the power to abolish all forms of human poverty and all forms of human life. And yet the same revolutionary beliefs for which our fore-bears fought are still at issue around the globe — the belief that the rights of man come not from the generosity of the state but from the hand of God.

We dare not forget today that we are the heirs of that first revolution. Let the word go forth from this time and place, to friend and foe alike, that the torch has been passed to a new generation of Americans—born in this century, tempered by war, disciplined by a hard and bitter peace, proud of our ancient heritage—and unwilling to witness or permit the slow undoing of those human rights to which this nation has always been committed, and to which we are committed today at home and around the world.

We are the heirs of that first revolution . . .

Let every nation know, whether it wishes us well or ill, that we shall pay any price, bear any burden, meet any hardship, support any friend, oppose any foe to assure the survival and the success of liberty.

This much we pledge—and more.

To those old allies whose cultural and spiritual origins we share, we pledge the loyalty of faithful friends. United, there is little we cannot do in a host of cooperative ventures. Divided, there is little we can do—for we dare not meet a powerful challenge at odds and split asunder.

To those new states whom we welcome to the ranks of the free, we pledge our word that one form of colonial control shall not have passed away merely to be replaced by a far more iron tyranny. We shall not always expect to find them supporting our view. But we shall always hope to find them strongly supporting their own freedom—and to remember that, in the past, those who foolishly sought power by riding the back of the tiger ended up inside.

We shall pay any price . . . to assure

the survival of liberty . . .

If a free society cannot help the many who are poor,
it cannot save the few who are rich . . .

To those peoples in the huts and villages of half the globe struggling to break the bonds of mass misery, we pledge our best efforts to help them help themselves, for whatever period is required — not because the communists may be doing it, not because we seek their votes, but because it is right. If a free society cannot help the many who are poor, it cannot save the few who are rich.

To our sister republics south of the border . . . a special pledge to convert our good words into good deeds . . .

To our sister republics south of our border, we offer a special pledge — to convert our good words into good deeds — in a new alliance for progress — to assist free men and free governments in casting off the chains of poverty. But this peaceful revolution of hope cannot become the prey of hostile powers. Let all our neighbors know that we shall join with them to oppose aggression or subversion anywhere in the Americas. And let every other power know that this Hemisphere intends to remain the master of its own house.

THEY SHALL BEAT THEIR SWORDS INTO PLOWSHARES, AND THEIR SPEARS INTO PRUNING HOOKS; NATION SHALL NOT LIFT UP SWORD AGAINST NATION, NEITHER SHALL THEY LEARN WAR ANY MORE

To the United Nations . . . our pledge of support . . .

To that world assembly of sovereign states, the United Nations, our last best hope in an age where the instruments of war have far outpaced the instruments of peace, we renew our pledge of support—to prevent it from becoming merely a forum for invective—to strengthen its shield of the new and the weak—and to enlarge the area in which its writ may run.

Begin anew the quest for peace, before the dark
powers of destruction engulf all humanity . . .

Finally, to those nations who would make themselves our adversary, we offer not a pledge but a request: that both sides begin anew the quest for peace, before the dark powers of destruction unleashed by science engulf all humanity in planned or accidental self-destruction.

We dare not tempt them with weakness. For only when our arms are sufficient beyond doubt can we be certain beyond doubt that they will never be employed.

But neither can two great and powerful groups of nations take comfort from our present course—both sides overburdened by the cost of modern weapons, both rightly alarmed by the steady spread of the deadly atom, yet both racing to alter that uncertain balance of terror that stays the hand of mankind's final war.

So let us begin anew — remembering on both sides that civility is not a sign of weakness, and sincerity is always subject to proof. Let us never negotiate out of fear. But let us never fear to negotiate.

Let both sides explore what problems unite us instead of belaboring those problems which divide us.

Let both sides, for the first time, formulate serious and precise proposals for the inspection and control of arms — and bring the absolute power to destroy other nations under the absolute control of all nations.

Let both sides seek to invoke the wonders of science instead of its terrors. Together let us explore the stars, conquer the deserts, eradicate disease, tap the ocean depths and encourage the arts and commerce.

Let both sides unite to heed in all corners of the earth the command of Isaiah — to "undo the heavy burdens . . . (and) let the oppressed go free."

And if a beach-head of cooperation may push back the jungle of suspicion, let both sides join in creating a new endeavor, not a new balance of power, but a new world of law, where the strong are just and the weak secure and the peace preserved.

And this will not be finished in the first one hundred days. Nor will it be finished in the first one thousand days, nor in the life of this Administration, nor even perhaps in our lifetime on this planet. But let us begin.

Let us ne

ear to negotiate . . .

Each generation ... has given testimony to its national loyalty ...

In your hands, my fellow citizens, more than mine, will rest the final success or failure of our course. Since this country was founded, each generation of Americans has been summoned to give testimony to its national loyalty. The graves of young Americans who answered the call to service surround the globe.

Now the trumpet summons us . . . to a struggle against
the common enemies of man . . .

Now the trumpet summons us again—not as a call to bear arms, though arms we need—not as a call to battle, though embattled we are—but a call to bear the burden of a long twilight struggle, year in and year out, "rejoicing in hope, patient in tribulation"—a struggle against the common enemies of man: tyranny, poverty, disease and war itself.

Can we forge against these enemies a grand and global alliance, North and South, East and West, that can assure a more fruitful life for all mankind? Will you join in that historic effort?

In the long history of the world, only a few generations have been granted the role of defending freedom in its hour of maximum danger. I do not shrink from this responsibility—I welcome it. I do not believe that any of us would exchange places with any other people or any other generation. The energy, the faith, the devotion which we bring to this endeavor will light our country and all who serve it—and the glow from that fire can truly light the world.

And so, my fellow Americans: ask not what your country can do for you—ask what you can do for your country.

Ask not what your country can do for you — ask what

you can do for your country . . .

My fellow citizens of the world: ask not what
America will do for you, but what together we can
do for the freedom of man.

Finally, whether you are citizens of America or citizens of the world, ask of us here the same high standards of strength and sacrifice which we ask of you. With a good conscience our only sure reward, with history the final judge of our deeds, let us go forth to lead the land we love, asking His blessing and His help, but knowing that here on earth God's work must truly be our own.

Ask of us here the same high standards of

strength and sacrifice which we ask of you ...

The White House

By the President of the United States of America

A PROCLAMATION

To the People of the United States:

John Fitzgerald Kennedy, thirty-fifth President of the United States, has been taken from us by an act which outrages decent men everywhere.

He upheld the faith of our fathers, which is freedom for all men. He broadened the frontiers of that faith, and backed it with the energy and the courage which are the mark of the Nation he led.

A man of wisdom, strength, and peace, he moulded and moved the power of our Nation in the service of a world of growing liberty and order. All who love freedom will mourn his death.

As he did not shrink from his responsibilities, but welcomed them, so he would not have us shrink from carrying on his work beyond this hour of national tragedy.

He said it himself: "The energy, the faith, the devotion which we bring to this endeavor will light our country and all who serve it —— and the glow from that fire can truly light the world."

Now, therefore, I, Lyndon B. Johnson, President of the United States of America, do appoint Monday next, November 25, the day of the funeral service of President Kennedy, to be a national day of mourning throughout the United States. I earnestly recommend the people to assemble on that day in their respective places of divine worship, there to bow down in submission to the will of Almighty God, and to pay their homage of love and reverence to the memory of a great and good man. I invite the people of the world who share our grief to join us in this day of mourning and rededication.

IN WITNESS WHEREOF, I have hereunto set my hand and caused the Seal of the United States of America to be affixed.

DONE at the City of Washington this twenty-third day of

 November in the year of our Lord nineteen hundred and sixty-three, and of the Independence of the United States of America the one hundred and eighty-eighth.

LYNDON B. JOHNSON

By the President:

DEAN RUSK

Secretary of State

Leonard Everett Fisher was born in New York City and received his Bachelor and Master of Fine Arts degrees at the Yale Art School. He has been awarded the Weir Prize, the Winchester Fellowship, and the Pulitzer Art Prize. In recent years he has become an extremely successful and sought—after illustrator of children's books. Among the books he has illustrated are The First Book of New England, The First Book of the Constitution, The First Book Edition of The Man Without a Country, The First Book Edition of The Declaration of Independence, The First Book Edition of A Message to Garcia, The First Book Edition of The Gettysburg Address and Second Inaugural, The First Book Edition of Paul Revere's Ride, America, America, America, and Patriotism, Patriotism, Patriotism.